Chinese Proverbs

This edition published in 2012 by

CHARTWELL BOOKS, INC.
A division of
BOOK SALES, INC.
276 Fifth Avenue Suite 206
New York, New York 10001
USA

ISBN: 978-0-7858-2982-9

Text: James Trapp
Project Editor: Michael Spilling
Design: Rajdip Sanghera

Printed and bound in China

TRADITIONAL CHINESE BOOKBINDING
This book has been produced using traditional Chinese bookbinding
techniques, using a method that was developed during the Ming Dynasty
(1368–1644) and remained in use until the adoption of Western binding
techniques in the early 1900s. In traditional Chinese binding, single sheets of
paper are printed on one side only, and each sheet is folded in half, with the
printed pages on the outside. The book block is then sandwiched between
two boards and sewn together through punched holes close to the cut edges
of the folded sheets.

Chinese Proverbs

成中
語國

THE WISDOM OF CHENG-YU

CHARTWELL
BOOKS, INC.

Introduction

成語, *chéngyǔ* in standard pinyin transliteration and pronounced *chung ewe*, literally translates as "become a saying" or more idiomatically "set phrase". They usually consist of four characters, though there is one chengyu in this collection with five characters. Chengyu add a depth and richness of expression to modern Chinese, which quite often is difficult to fully translate. English, too, has its own proverbs and idioms. These serve much the same function but they do not have the same standard format as chengyu and they are not as commonly used.

   Chengyu are immediately recognizable, and not just because of their format. They are usually next to impossible to understand if you don't know the story behind them. This is because a whole anecdote is condensed into four characters, often using words and grammar from Classical Chinese no longer in current usage. Both

dǎ tiě chèn rè
(pronounced *da tieh chen rerr*)
Literal meaning: hit iron still hot
Idiomatic meaning: strike while the iron is hot

āi bīng bì shèng

(pronounced *eye bing bee shung*)

Literal meaning: sorrowing army must win

Idiomatic meaning: justice will prevail

The philosopher Lao Zi (c. sixth century BCE) author of the Dao De Jing, the principal text of Daoism, first expressed the sentiment of this chengyu. It is perhaps not immediately apparent why a "sorrowing" army must be guaranteed victory. In fact "sorrowing", which is the direct translation of the character 哀, really has to be expanded into "grieving with righteous indignation over an injustice". This shows just how much meaning a single character can carry.

of these things contribute to their effectiveness when used correctly, but if you are a foreigner you cannot be expected to comprehend them.

Some chengyu do not have a historical story attached to them and are just clever ways of expressing a common sentiment. However, almost all of the chengyu included in this collection refer back to stories found in some of the earliest Chinese literature. Many of these sources stem from either famous Chinese philosophers, such as Confucius and Zhuangzi, or historical records, particularly of the period known as the Warring States (476–221 BCE), when China was almost constantly caught up in civil war. Gaining a familiarity of chengyu does not just improve one's spoken Chinese, but it also gives an insight into the richness and variety of Chinese history and tradition.

qián lǘ jì qióng
(pronounced *chien lew jee chiung*)
Literal meaning: Qian donkey exhausts tricks
Idiomatic meaning: have one's bluff called; to run out of excuses

bān mén nòng fǔ

(pronounced *ban mun noong foo*)

Literal meaning: Ban's door use axe

Idiomatic meaning: teach your grandmother to suck eggs

Lu Ban was a semi-legendary craftsman who was highly skilled with the axe. This chengyu was first used to describe aspiring poets who once visited the tomb of the great Tang Dynasty poet Li Bai (701–762) and left inscriptions of their own poems on the rocks around it. The Ming scholar Mei Zhihuan said this was like "showing off with an axe outside Lu Ban's door". This saying can either be used to criticize someone else's actions, or to politely belittle one's own efforts in comparison to another's.

bàn tú ér fèi

(pronounced *ban too ahr fay*)

Literal meaning: half road then stop

Idiomatic meaning: give up too easily; leave something half done;
if it's worth doing, it's worth doing well

This comes from a parable told by a grandson of Confucius, the philosopher Zisi (481–402 BCE), in his book *The Doctrine of the Mean*. A man went off to the city to study, but decided it was too difficult and came home after only a year. His wife was very cross with him. She had been weaving a piece of fine cloth for many months and on her husband's return she cut it into pieces. He asked her why she had wasted so many months' work. She replied that it was just the same as him giving up his studies halfway through. If something is worth doing you must be prepared to spend time on it.

bēi gōng shé yǐng

(pronounced *bay goong sher ying*)

Literal meaning: glass bow snake image

Idiomatic meaning: start at shadows; always be looking over your shoulder

This is one of those chengyu that is completely incomprehensible until it is explained. A man hadn't seen one of his friends for some time, and heard from another acquaintance that the friend was too scared to return after his last visit. Apparently he had seen the reflection of a snake in the cup of wine he had been drinking, and was afraid the snake might still be there. After some thought the man realized that the reflection of a bow hanging on his wall might have been caught on the surface of the wine and looked like a snake, so he immediately reassured his friend.

bī shàng liáng shān

(pronounced *bee shang liang shan*)

Literal meaning: forced to climb Mount Liang

Idiomatic meaning: necessity is the mother of invention; take the only possible course of action; be driven to extremes

The marshes around Mount Liang in Shandong province, North China, are renowned for being the home of the bandits and outlaws made famous in the first great Chinese novel 水滸傳 shuǐ hǔ zhuàn. The novel, best known in English as *The Water Margin*, was written in the fourteenth century. It tells the stories of 108 heroes forced into hiding and exile by the injustices of local government under the Song Dynasty (960–1279). The heroes are the Chinese equivalent of Robin Hood and his Merry Men and some of the characters are the most popular in Chinese literature.

chén yú luò yàn

(pronounced *chun yew law yen*)
Literal meaning: sink fish drop goose
Idiomatic meaning: drop-dead gorgeous; super-model looks

This chengyu combines stories about two different historical beauties. The first lived in the seventh century BCE and was a concubine sent as a gift from the king of Yue to the king of Wu. It was said of her that when the fish in the river saw her they swam to hide at the bottom because they felt so ugly. The second beauty lived during the Han Dynasty (206 BCE–220 CE) and was also being sent as a tribute. A goose flying overhead saw the woman while she was on her way. The bird was so entranced by her looks that it flew straight into a tree.

dǎ cǎo jīng shé

(pronounced *da tsow jing sher*)

Literal meaning: beat grass warn snake

Idiomatic meaning: give the game away; tip someone off

This is an old story from Anhui province in central China. There was once a corrupt official called Wang Lu who often took bribes and embezzled money. He was aided and abetted by his equally corrupt secretary. One day a local man came to the court to lay charges against the secretary. These charges were too close to home for Wang Lu's liking and he became very agitated. He was so distracted that instead of writing down his judgement in the case, he wrote the words 打草惊蛇. After this scare, he took extra care to cover his tracks in future.

dǎ tiě chèn rè

(pronounced *da tieh chen rerr*)
Literal meaning: hit iron still hot
Idiomatic meaning: strike while the iron is hot

The fascinating thing about this particular saying is the way that exactly the same metaphor is used by two cultures widely separated by time and distance. There is no question of this reflecting any contact between Chinese and English-speaking communities. Instead, it is an illustration of the importance of the ironsmith's craft in early societies and the powerful imagery it provoked. (The Chinese were also the inventors of the blast furnace for the sophisticated production of iron, beating the West by more than 1500 years.)

有盗道亦

dào yì yǒu dào

(pronounced *dow yee yo dow*)

Literal meaning: thieves also have their Dao

Idiomatic meaning: there is honour among thieves

This is an elegantly balanced saying, which employs a clever play on words between the first and fourth characters. Each is pronounced exactly the same way but the meaning of the first, "thief" or "robber" contrasts strongly with the final character, which is the "Dao" of the philosophy Daoism, meaning the True Way or the Path of All Things. Although the English translation "honour among thieves" serves adequately at one level, there is a deeper meaning in the Chinese, suggesting that there is a spiritually true way of doing anything, even thieving.

dōng chuāng shì fā

(pronounced *doong farng shrrr far*)

Literal meaning: east window affair exposed

Idiomatic meaning: the game is up; one's cover is blown; all is known

The story behind this chengyu comes from a novel written during the Ming Dynasty (1368–1644) and has beautiful women, betrayal and ghosts – everything a good story needs. At the beginning of the twelfth century China was being invaded by nomads from the north. A treacherous general and his beautiful wife hatched a plot to lure away a loyal commander from his post to let the nomads in. The false general died soon after and was sent to undergo terrible punishment in the Underworld. From there he sent his wife a dream warning her that the plot they hatched "under the east window" was known, and that she should flee.

duì niú tán qín

(pronounced *dway nee-oh tan chin*)

Literal meaning: towards ox play lute

Idiomatic meaning: cast pearls before swine; not pick one's audience

There are differing versions of this story, one considerably older than the other. In the latter version, the musician plays beautiful music to an ox and cannot understand why the ox is unmoved by it. In the end he decides it is because the ox is stupid and unrefined. The earlier version is a serious Buddhist parable in which in the musician realizes that the ox does not understand the music he is playing so he starts playing sounds the ox can recognize. The ox immediately pays attention. The lesson here is that Buddhist teachings need to be explained in terms of Chinese understanding, not just translated straight from the original.

難覆
收水

fù shuǐ nán shōu

(pronounced *foo shwei nan show*)

Literal meaning: upset water hard to gather

Idiomatic meaning: it's no use crying over spilt milk; you can't undo what is done

The origins of this saying are obscure, but one version goes back to the Shang Dynasty (1723–1046 BCE). General Jiang Taigong retired from official life disgusted by the cruelty of the emperor. His wife was unhappy with the loss of status and became estranged from her husband. He protested that they would one day be rich again but she did not believe him. Soon, the Shang Dynasty was overthrown and Jiang took a new post under the Zhou emperor. His wife tried to return but he threw a pot of water on the ground and told her they had the same chance of getting back together as of she had gathering up the water.

guā tián lǐ xià

(pronounced *gwa tien lee hsia*)

Literal meaning: melon field under plum tree

Idiomatic meaning: act suspiciously; don't draw attention to yourself

Emperor Wen of the Tang Dynasty (618–907) could not understand why people were suspicious of his appointment of a particular provincial governor. His advisers explained that when the official's daughters came to court to pay their respects to the emperor's mother, the people believed they had been offered as a bribe to the emperor. In welcoming them he had been like a man bending down in a melon patch to tie his shoe, or taking his cap off in a plum orchard to scratch his head. Both actions, though innocent, might look as though he was trying to steal the fruit.

hǎo shì duō mó

(pronounced *how shrr dor mor*)

Literal meaning: a good deed has many twists

Idiomatic meaning: nothing good is ever simple

This saying could well stand as an unofficial motto for the aspiring Confucian gentleman, even though it is not Confucian in origin. Confucius himself experienced many "twists of the grindstone" (the literal meaning of the character 磨) as he doggedly pursued his quest to find an enlightened ruler. Any of his followers who attempt properly to follow the path of 仁 and 义 (rén and yì, benevolence and righteousness) are sure to find the same.

hè lì jī qún

(pronounced *her lee gee chwoon*)

Literal meaning: crane standing in a crowd of chickens

Idiomatic meaning: standing out from the crowd;
head and shoulders above the rest

Some chengyu are simply similes that have been in common use for a long time. Often there are stories attached about when they were first used, or the most important example of their use. In this case the phrase supposedly refers back to the admiring description of a noble and talented minister called Ji Shao who refused to desert his master Jin Hui, emperor of the Jin Dynasty (1115–1234), when he was defeated in battle.

hòu lái jū shàng

(pronounced *hoe lie joo shang*)

Literal meaning: late arrive stay top

Idiomatic meaning: Johnny come lately; jump the queue; go straight to the top

This old chengyu is first found in the *Records of the Grand Historian* written by Sima Qian in the second century BCE. It is interesting because its use has changed over time. Originally it was used by Sima Qian to describe criticism of an emperor who promoted newcomers who flattered him over those with age and experience: "Like piling up firewood you put the new stuff on top." Nowadays it is more likely to be used to express admiration of someone who gets to the top of his or her profession while still very young.

hǔ fù hǔ zǐ

(pronounced *hoo foo hoo dze*)

Literal meaning: if the father is a tiger the son will be a tiger

Idiomatic meaning: like father like son; chip off the old block

The tiger enjoys a special place in the Chinese consciousness. The South China or Amoy tiger, of which few remain in the wild, is generally considered to be the evolutionary ancestor of all tigers. Its endangered status is due both to destruction of its habitat and to the fact that every part of its body finds a use in traditional Chinese medicine. It is also the third animal in the Chinese zodiac. Given the tiger's status, this saying would normally be used in a complimentary rather than derogatory way.

hǔ tóu shé wěi

(pronounced *hoo toe sher way*)

Literal meaning: head of a tiger tail of a snake

Idiomatic meaning: in like a lion, out like a lamb

At first sight this saying might suggest something monstrous, strange and terrifying but in fact it is the reverse. The tiger, as one of the most important animals in the Chinese bestiary, stands for magnificence and splendour. However, the snake's tail, which is plain and smooth and tapers away, represents letdown and disappointment. In chapter 103 of the famous Ming Dynasty novel *The Water Margin* it is used to describe local government affairs: all urgency at the start tailing off into inactivity. This proverb also exists in the form "head of a dragon, tail of a snake".

hú lún tūn zǎo

(pronounced *who lun twun dzow*)

Literal meaning: whole swallow dates

Idiomatic meaning: a little learning is a dangerous thing; learn something parrot-fashion without actually understanding it

A doctor told his patient that eating dates would be a good cure for his spleen problem, but that he needed to be careful of eating too many as chewing them could damage his teeth. The patient replied that there was no problem. He would simply swallow them whole without chewing. What he did not realize was that this would cause him stomach problems and make his spleen worse. Learning by rote has been the basis of Chinese education for many centuries (though of course that is changing now), so "swallowing dates whole" was a constant danger.

虎狐威假

hú jiǎ hǔ wēi

(pronounced *who jar who way*)

Literal meaning: fox fakes tiger's power

Idiomatic meaning: ride on someone's coat-tails; hide behind authority

In another ancient fable, a tiger catches a fox and is about to eat him. The fox cries out to stop the tiger, claiming that the Jade Emperor chose him, the fox, as the leader of all the beasts. At first the tiger doesn't believe him, but the fox says he can prove it. He suggests they go for a walk through the jungle with the fox in the lead, and the tiger will see that all the other animals are in awe of him and run away. Of course the animals all run away but only because they can see the tiger behind the fox.

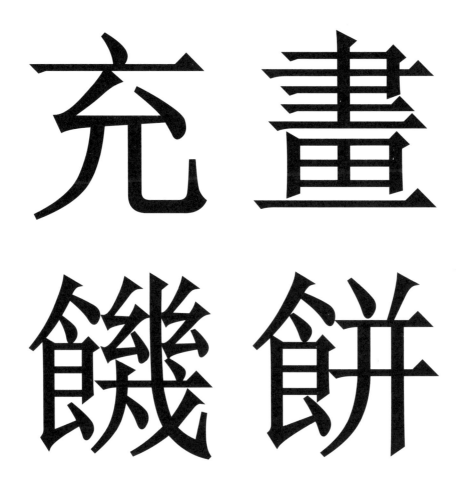

huà bǐng chōng jī

(pronounced *hwa bing choong gee*)

Literal meaning: paint cake satisfy hunger

Idiomatic meaning: all bangs and whistles; all show but no effect; a token effort of no practical use

This is another example of where the story behind a chengyu does not really explain its origins but simply associates its use with a famous person. Like many others, this dates back to the Warring States period (476–221 BCE). At that time Lu Yu was a trusted adviser to the king of Wei and had reached his position through merit, not family connections. The King trusted him particularly because of this, and often complained that most of his other officials had got their posts through connections and not competence, which was like drawing a cake to satisfy one's hunger.

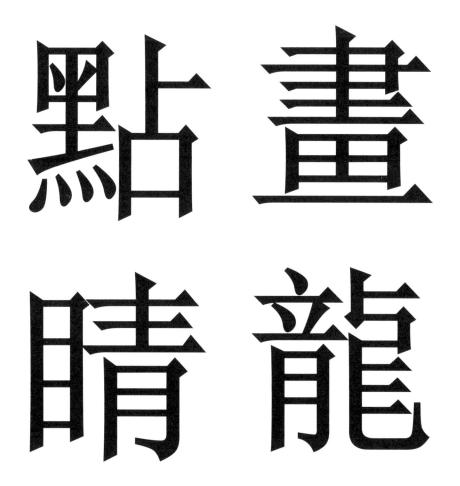

huà lóng diǎn jīng

(pronounced *hwa long dyen jing*)

Literal meaning: paint dragon add eyes

Idiomatic meaning: a detail that makes all the difference; bring something
to life; the finishing touch

This chengyu concerns a real artist called Zhang Sengyao, who lived in the early sixth century. He was commissioned to paint four dragons on the wall of a monastery. When he had finished, everyone admired the painting, saying how life-like the dragons looked. They noticed, however, that Zhang had not finished the eyes on any of the dragons. When they asked him why not, he replied that if he put in the eyes the dragons really would come to life. No one believed him, so he applied the final strokes to two of the dragons. There was an almighty peal of thunder and the two dragons flew away, leaving behind only the two with unfinished eyes.

huà shé tiān zú

(pronounced *hwa sher tien dzoo*)

Literal meaning: paint snake add legs

Idiomatic meaning: gild the lily; overegg the pudding

The story behind this common saying, which describes spoiling something by going too far or trying too hard, first appears in the *Zhan Guo Ce*, historical records written in the third century BCE. Supposedly a group of friends were having a painting competition to see who could produce a painting of a snake in the shortest time. The prize was a jar of wine. One artist was so much quicker than the others that he decided to show off and add something extra. He painted some legs on his snake, but when he tried to claim the wine, his friends disqualified him because his painting was no longer that of a snake.

jiāo bīng bì bài

(pronounced *jao bing bee bye*)

Literal meaning: an arrogant army will always lose

Idiomatic meaning: pride goes before a fall

This is a saying that truly spans the centuries and the globe. Although it sounds as though it should be (and would not be out of place there), it is not a quotation from Sunzi's famous work *The Art of War*. The earliest version of it appears in the *Han Shu* (History of the Former Han Dynasty), written at the end of the second century BCE. In a very different context, a Republican Congressman writing in the *Washington Times* in March 2008, quoted it as a warning to the United States not to be complacent over China.

jié căo xián huán

(pronounced *ji-air tsow hsien hwan*)

Literal meaning: knot grass carry ring

Idiomatic meaning: one good deed deserves another; repay a debt of kindness

There are two stories behind this chengyu. In the first a man is asked by his father to make sure his favourite concubine is looked after when he dies. On his deathbed, however, the father grows delirious and orders the concubine to commit suicide. The son remembers the first instruction and spares the girl. Later, in battle, the son is saved from death when an old man mysteriously appears and ties the grass in front of an attacking enemy's horse into a knot, tripping the horse. In a dream the old man reveals himself as the father of the concubine repaying his debt. In the second story, a man saves an injured sparrow, which later returns with a jade ring in its beak.

jǐng dǐ zhī wā

(pronounced *jing dee jrrr wah*)

Literal meaning: frog at the bottom of a well

Idiomatic meaning: used to describe someone narrow-minded
and not open to new ideas

This chengyu refers to a parable from the works of the fourth-century BCE Daoist philosopher Zhuangzi. In this tale, a frog is sitting happily in a small pond at the bottom of a well. A sea turtle is passing the well and looks down into it. The frog calls up to the turtle to come and join him, as he is completely happy in the best of all possible homes.

The turtle suggests instead that the frog come up and join him in returning to the ocean, which is far bigger and finer than the frog's pond. The frog cannot understand how this is possible, and stays where he is.

jiǔ niú yī máo

(pronounced *joe nee-oh eee mao*)

Literal meaning: nine oxen one hair

Idiomatic meaning: of no importance; insignificant

Many chengyu come from or are found in the works of Sima Qian (146–86 BCE), regarded as Chinese historiography. But this one is actually about him. Sima Qian was good friends with the Han general Li Ling, and when Li was accused of treason, Sima defended him. For this, Sima found himself in the disfavour of the Emperor Wudi. He was condemned to death but begged for clemency so that he could finish his great historical work, even though, in his own words, it was "no more significant than the loss of one hair from nine oxen". Sima's life was spared but his punishment was castration.

辟開
地天

kāi tiān pì dì

(pronounced *kye tien pee dee*)

Literal meaning: open heaven break the earth

Idiomatic meaning: advance by leaps and bounds; take giant strides;
make a super-human effort

In the traditional Chinese creation myth, at first earth and heaven were bound together like a
huge egg. In this egg lived a giant called Pan Gu. Eighteen thousand years after the beginning
of creation, Pan Gu started to separate heaven from earth as though separating the white
from the yolk. This task took him another 18,000 years, and after he had finished he died of
exhaustion. This chengyu is now used to describe something achieved with huge effort, or
great progress being made in an important endeavour.

kè zhōu qiú jiàn

(pronounced *cur joe chee-oh jen*)

Literal meaning: carve boat to look for sword

Idiomatic meaning: be behind the times; not keep up with changes

This story first appears in the *Spring and Autumn Annals*, one of the five classics of Chinese literature traditionally believed to have been written by Confucius. It is a saying particularly relevant to modern times, where knowledge and technology are advancing so quickly. It illustrates the dangers of falling behind the times. A man is crossing a river in a boat when he drops his sword overboard. Instead of stopping and diving to find it immediately, he marks the side of the boat where the sword fell and then tries to find it when he reaches the other side.

kǒng róng ràng lí

(pronounced *koong roong rang lee*)

Literal meaning: Kong Rong allows a pear

Idiomatic meaning: no direct equivalent, used to praise a virtuous child;
perhaps "wise beyond his/her years"

This saying comes from a folk-tale about a young boy called Kong Rong. He had five elder brothers and one younger. One day the family was given a gift of a bowl of pears. When told that he could have first choice, Kong Rong chose the smallest one. His father asked him why he didn't take a larger one and he replied that he should leave those for his elder brothers, as they were senior to him. "But you have a younger brother," said his father, "Don't you deserve a bigger one than him?"

"No," replied Kong Rong, "I am his elder brother and I should look after him."

kū yú zhī sì

(pronounced *coo ewe jrrr srrr*)

Literal meaning: dried fish store

Idiomatic meaning: jam tomorrow is no use now; if wishes were horses beggars would ride

A man went to borrow some money from a friend, but the friend told him he could not lend any until the end of the month. The man was upset and told his friend that on the way over he had seen a carp writhing in a dried-up pond. The carp had begged him to bring water immediately but the man had said he would bring some back after he had seen his friend. The carp replied that in that case the man had better look for him in the dried-fish shop, because it would be too late. "Now," said the man to his friend, "you are doing the same thing to me!"

làn yú chōng shù

(pronounced *lan ewe choong shoo*)

Literal meaning: extra flute make up numbers

Idiomatic meaning: there just to make up the numbers; a make-weight

The Legalist philosopher Han Fei (280–233 BCE) told this story. A "yu" is a traditional Chinese wind instrument. King Xuan of Qi particularly loved the music of the yu and assembled an orchestra for his entertainment. A poor man saw his chance to get free food and accommodation by infiltrating the orchestra even though he couldn't play. The king only liked ensemble pieces, so the man got away with his deception. However, when King Xuan died and his son took over, the man was in trouble. The new king only liked solo pieces and ordered each musician to play in turn. Rather than be found out, the man ran away.

láng bèi wéi jiān

(pronounced *lang bay way jen*)

Literal meaning: long-legged wolf and short-legged wolf make mischief

Idiomatic meaning: partners in crime; be in cahoots together

For this saying to work we have to believe that there are two types of wolf, the 狼 (láng), which is a normal wolf with long front legs and shorter hind legs and the 狽 (bèi), a strange variant with front legs shorter than its hind legs. These beasts were out hunting one day and came to a sheep pen with a high fence. The "lang" stood on the shoulders of the "bei", which stretched up on its long hind legs. The "lang" then reached out with its long front legs and caught a lamb each for their dinner.

liáng shàng jūn zǐ

(pronounced *leeang shang june dze*)

Literal meaning: gentleman on the roof-beam
Idiomatic meaning: thief; housebreaker

A story is told of the Later Han scholar Chen Shi, who lived at the end of the second century. He was sitting in his house with his sons when he noticed a thief hiding up in the roof-beams. He pretended not to see him at first but turned the subject of discussion with his sons to life and work. He praised his sons for all being hard working and conscientious but went on to say that they would meet some people who, although not bad in themselves, turned to crime because they did not like working. At this he pointed to the thief in the rafters, called him down and gave him money to go away and set himself up in business.

luò yáng zhǐ guì

(pronounced *law yang jrrr gway*)

Literal meaning: Luoyang paper expensive

Idiomatic meaning: a bestseller; selling like hot cakes (of a book)

Luoyang in Henan province is one of the Seven Ancient Capitals of China. Living there in the third century was a famous writer called Zuo Si. He decided to write a history of the capital cities of the Three Kingdoms. Other writers mocked him and said it would never sell. Nonetheless Zuo Si stuck to his task, and when the book was finished it became hugely popular. Everybody wanted to own a copy of the book. In those days the only way was to buy paper, brushes and ink and make a copy for one's self. So many people did so that the price of paper in Luoyang shot up.

luò yè guī gēn

(pronounced *law yeah gwei gun*)

Literal meaning: fall leaf return root

Idiomatic meaning: leaves don't fall far from the tree; there's no place like home

This is a very poignant saying that refers particularly to the millions of Chinese who, over the centuries, have had to move away from their ancestral home. In past times it was those adventurous spirits who travelled across the globe and established Chinese communities all over the world. Nowadays, it may be even more applicable to the waves of people leaving the countryside to find work in the cities. For all of them, as they grow old or ill, their thoughts turn to returning to their 老家 (lǎo jiā) or "old home".

máng rén mō xiàng

(pronounced *mang wren more hsiang*)

Literal meaning: blind men feeling an elephant

Idiomatic meaning: not see the wood for the trees; unable to see the whole picture

This is originally a Buddhist parable illustrating how hard it is for one man to see the whole truth of the Buddha's teachings. Five blind men are examining an elephant to try to understand what it is like. The first one feels the elephant's tusk and says: "An elephant is like a large smooth radish." The second feels the elephant's ear and decides it is like a giant dustpan. The third feels its back and says it must be like a bed, and so on. This saying also serves to illustrate the importance of working together and sharing knowledge.

Máo Suì zì jiàn

(pronounced *mao sway dzrr jien*)

Literal meaning: Mao Sui self praise

Idiomatic meaning: don't hide your light under a bushel; blow your own trumpet; don't be backward in coming forward

This story is found in the *Shi Ji* (*Records of the Grand Historian*) written by Sima Qian (146–86 BCE). The king of Chu was sending military advisers to help Zhao against the king of Qin. Mao Sui stepped forward and demanded his inclusion in the group. The king asked how it was that no one at court had heard of him before, since talent, like an awl in a leather bag, will always show through. Mao Sui replied that his awl had not yet been put in the king's bag, but if it were it would soon break through. The king was impressed by Mao's confidence and allowed him to join the group.

míng luò Sūn Shān

(pronounced *ming law soon shan*)

Literal meaning: name below Sun Shan

Idiomatic meaning: a tactful way of telling someone they have failed an examination or test

During the Song Dynasty (960–1279) a young scholar called Sun Shan was travelling up to the capital to take the civil service examinations. One of his neighbours begged him to take his young son with him so he too could sit the exams. When the results were published, Sun Shan's name was the very last on the list of successful candidates and the neighbour's son's did not appear. When they returned to their village and the neighbour asked how his son had done, Sun Shan tactfully did not say outright that he had failed, but replied, "His name was below mine on the list."

mó chǔ chéng zhēn

(pronounced *more choo chung jun*)

Literal meaning: grind stick to become needle

Idiomatic meaning: slow and steady wins the race; slowly but surely;

never say die

This saying comes from a story about the famous Tang Dynasty poet Li Bai (701–762). When out on the road one day, Li Bai saw an old man sitting on the ground holding an iron bar. Li Bai asked him what he was doing with the bar. "I am going to grind it down to make a needle," the old man replied. Li Bai was so impressed by the old man's dedication that he resolved to take up the studies he had abandoned through lack of application. In fact, he never did, but that rather spoils the point of the saying.

nán yuán běi zhé

(pronounced *nan ewe-an bay jer*)

Literal meaning: south chariot shafts north wheel tracks

Idiomatic meaning: get in one's own way; hinder one's own efforts;
shoot one's self in the foot

This story is told in the *Zhan Guo Ce* (*Strategies of the Warring States*) written some time in the third century BCE. The king of Wei was planning to attack Zhao, but one of his advisors, believing it would be counterproductive, counselled him against this plan. He told the king he had just met a traveller who said he was heading south, but his chariot was pointing north. When asked why this should be, the man said he had money and time to waste so it didn't matter to him. The king, however, could not afford this luxury.

niú jiǎo guà shū

(pronounced *nee-oh jee-ow gwa shoo*)

Literal meaning: ox horns hang books

Idiomatic meaning: said of a really hard-working student; be a bookworm

The origins of the story behind this chengyu are not clear, but it concerns a boy called Li Mi. He was very hard worker and keen to improve himself, so he spent all his spare time reading and studying. One day his father sent him off on a long journey, and, in order not to waste a moment's study time, he took all his books with him and hung them on the horns of the ox he was riding. A famous scholar spotted him reading on the ox's back and praised him lavishly for his studious ways.

pò fǔ chén zhōu

(pronounced *por foo chun joe*)

Literal meaning: break cauldrons burn boats

Idiomatic meaning: burn one's bridges; pass the point of no return; go all in

The story behind this saying appears in both Sunzi's *Art of War* and Sima Qian's *Records of the Grand Historian*. As the king of Qin was setting out to conquer all the other states and unify China, his army invaded the state of Zhao and besieged a city beside the River Zhang. A general from the neighbouring state of Chu, called Xiang Yu, led his army to the aid the city. Once they had crossed the River Zhang he ordered his troops to smash their cooking pots and burn their boats, so they could not eat or retreat until they had defeated the Qin army.

pò jìng chóng yuán

(pronounced *por jing choong yew-an*)

Literal meaning: broken mirror again round

Idiomatic meaning: said of a couple reunited after a long separation; together again at last

An official was married to the daughter of the king, but the two of them were nervous about the future because the king took little care of state affairs. The husband broke a bronze mirror in half and the couple promised each other that if they were separated, they would each bring their half to a certain place at a certain time. Sure enough the kingdom fell and the two were separated. The new king took the woman as his concubine and kept her captive. Nonetheless she managed to send her servant with the mirror to the appointed spot where her husband found her. The king took pity on their devotion and allowed them to be reunited.

qǐ rén yōu tiān

(pronounced *chee wren yo tien*)

Literal meaning: man from Qi worries about the sky

Idiomatic meaning: don't worry about things you can't control

This chengyu is taken from a story in the *Liezi*, a Daoist text of the fifth century BCE. It is a simple admonition to let go of false worries and concerns and tells of a man from the state of Qi who was always afraid lest the sky should fall in. He used to go around pestering his friends and neighbours about what they should do if that happened. They all tried to reassure him that the sky was not like a roof and could not fall, but he never quite believed them and lived his life in a state of constant fear.

技黔
窮驢

qián lǘ jì qióng

(pronounced *chien lew jee chiung*)

Literal meaning: Qian donkey exhausts tricks

Idiomatic meaning: have one's bluff called; to run out of excuses

This is a story told by the Tang Dynasty author Liu Zongyuan (773–819). In the state of Qian (modern Guizhou) donkeys were unknown, so when a merchant arrived with one, it was an object of great interest. A local tiger was particularly interested. At first it treated this large grey animal with caution, and ran away whenever the donkey saw it and let out a loud bray. Gradually, the tiger grew bolder and went right up to the donkey. The donkey kicked out and the tiger ran away again, but when it realized that the donkey's kick had not really hurt, it went back and ate the donkey.

qiǎng cí duó lǐ

(pronounced *chiang tsrr dor lee*)

Literal meaning: strain words struggle reason

Idiomatic meaning: quibble over detail; split hairs; nitpick

Originally this chengyu was used to mean someone who took up an unreasonable position and was unwilling to move from it. The story tells of a man who loved to debate and would argue over anything. He wanted to build a new house but the carpenter told him the wood was too wet and he should wait. The man disagreed saying that, in fact, wet wood made stronger houses and insisted they continue. The house was built, and of course the wood cracked and gave way. Nowadays the saying is used for anyone who is pedantic or tries to be too clever.

qīng chū yú lán

(pronounced *ching chew you lan*)

Literal meaning: indigo dye comes from the indigo plant

Idiomatic meaning: the pupil surpasses the master; the present improves on the past; standing on the shoulders of giants

This chengyu is used by, among others, the great Tang Dynasty poet Bai Juyi (772–846). It comes from a story about the teacher Gong Fan and his student Li Mi. Li used all his time to study the teachings of his master and to extend his knowledge even further. Eventually Gong recognized that his student has surpassed him and would often himself consult Li if he had a problem. Li was very embarrassed until Gong, using this analogy, explained that this was the correct order of things, and that he was not upset to have educated Gong so well that he had been exceeded by his own pupil.

qū tū xǐ xīn

(pronounced *chew too see sin*)

Literal meaning: bend chimney move firewood

Idiomatic meaning: avoid trouble before it starts; better safe than sorry

This is a traditional tale from the Han Dynasty (206 BCE–220 CE) and appears in the *Han Shu*, the official history of the period. A good neighbour tried to warn a householder of the danger he ran in keeping his firewood next to a simple straight chimney. He advised him to alter the chimney so that it had a bend in it to control the airflow, and to move his wood farther away. The householder ignored his advice, and one day his house burnt down. At first the man was cross with his neighbour, but the other villagers pointed out that it was his own fault because he had not followed good advice.

sài wēng shī mǎ

(pronounced *sigh wung shrr ma*)

Literal meaning: at the frontier old man loses horse

Idiomatic meaning: a blessing in disguise

The proverbs themselves often offer little clue to their meaning, and can only be understood if the background is known. This is a prime example. It refers to an ancient story in which an old man loses his horse, which returns in time with a second horse. Later, it throws the man's son, who breaks his leg. At first this seems a great tragedy, but later it allows him to dodge military conscription and avoid being caught in a terrible defeat in which he would have certainly died.

sān rén chéng hǔ

(pronounced *san wren chung hoo*)

Literal meaning: three people make a tiger

Idiomatic meaning: don't believe everything you hear; false rumours
are easily spread

This is another story from the Warring States period (476–221 BCE), a time of combat, trickery and political intrigue. A minister asks his king whether he would believe it if three people told him there was a tiger in the street, even though he knew there could not possibly be. The king replies that one or two people would not convince him, but three would, even though he knew it was impossible. The minister begged the king to remember this if he heard rumours about the minister while he was away on the king's business.

shā jī qǔ luǎn

(pronounced *shah gee chew lawn*)

Literal meaning: kill chicken take egg

Idiomatic meaning: kill the goose that lays the golden egg; make do with what you have

This is a much simpler Chinese version of the fairytale of the goose that laid the golden egg, and shares the same moral. A simpleton farmer is not content with just the one egg a day his chicken provides him with. So he cuts the chicken open, hoping to find an endless supply of eggs. Of course, he ends up with none. Rather strangely, along with this chengyu, there are at least three other sayings that begin 殺 雞: "kill a chicken to scare the monkeys", "kill a chicken with an ox knife" and "kill a chicken and make sweet-corn rice". The first two explain themselves and the third is the equivalent of "killing the fatted calf".

shí zhǐ dà dòng

(pronounced *shrrr jrrr da doong*)

Literal meaning: eating finger big movement

Idiomatic meaning: have a craving for (food)

Song and Jia worked as officials in the court of their king, but their main preoccupation was food. One day, on their way to the court, Song's forefinger began to twitch. "That means I'm going to eat well today!" he said. Sure enough, the king had just received a fine river turtle, which had been cooked for his lunch. Jia told the king about Song's finger and the king laughed and said, "We'll see about that!" When the turtle was served there was enough for everyone except Song. Undaunted, he reached across and took a piece of turtle from the king's bowl. "My finger never lies!" he said.

shǒu zhū dāi tù

(pronounced *show ju dye two*)

Literal meaning: guard tree stump wait for rabbit

Idiomatic meaning: don't trust to luck; there's no such thing as a free lunch

This is a favourite saying and has its origin in the third-century BCE philosophical work *Han Fei Zi*. A farmer is working in his fields when a rabbit runs straight into a tree stump and kills itself. The farmer takes the rabbit home for his supper. As he is eating it, he thinks to himself how easy it was getting the rabbit. He decides that he no longer needs to look after his crops. All he has to do is wait by the tree stump for more rabbits. Of course, no more rabbits run into the stump, and the farmer starves.

楚四歌面

sì miàn chǔ gē

(pronounced *srrr mien chew ger*)

Literal meaning: four sides Chu songs

Idiomatic meaning: in a tight spot; beset on all sides; surrounded

This is a story from a pivotal time in Chinese history at the end of the third century BCE. China was once again succumbing to civil war after the collapse of the Qin Dynasty (221–206 BCE) under the First Emperor. Two warlords, Liu Bang and Xiang Yu, were fighting it out for control. Liu Bang had Xiang Yu surrounded but couldn't press home his advantage. He ordered his troops to sing songs from the state of Chu, homeland of Xiang Yu's troops. This made them so homesick they surrendered and Liu Bang went on to found the great Han Dynasty (206 BCE–220 CE).

tān zì biàn pín

(pronounced *tan dzrr byen pin*)

Literal meaning: the character for greed becomes the character for poverty

Idiomatic meaning: greed and poverty are neighbours

To appreciate the subtlety of this saying requires knowledge of Chinese characters. As well as being the ideal language for verbal puns (because it has so many words that sound identical but have different meanings), written Chinese abounds in visual wordplay. Characters are formed of two constituent parts, the radical and the phonetic. Here the two characters 貪 and 貧 share the same radical 貝 and have phonetics 今 and 分 that look very similar. Thus it takes only a very slight alteration or mistake when writing them for one to turn into the other, in the same way being too greedy can easily tip you into poverty.

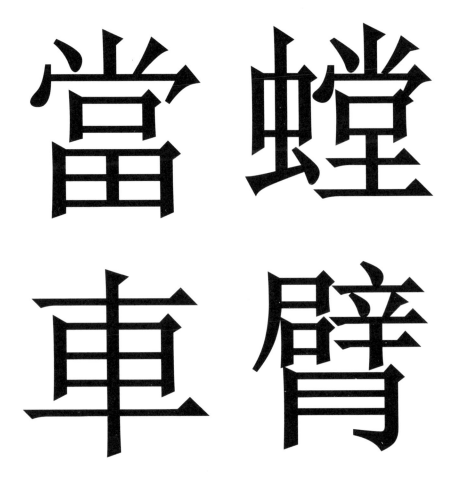

táng bì dāng chē

(pronounced *tang bee dang cher*)

Literal meaning: mantis legs stop chariot

Idiomatic meaning: David and Goliath; to be fearless; not be daunted by the size of a task or opponent

The mantis is an insect much admired by the Chinese for its courage and ferocity. Among others, the Daoist philosopher Zhuangzi (fourth century BCE) used this chengyu. The Duke of Qi was out hunting in his chariot when he saw a mantis on the road. He stopped his chariot to see what the insect would do. Instead of getting out of the way, the mantis marched on and grasped the wheel of the chariot as though determined to push it out of the way. The Duke was greatly impressed by this display of courage and determination.

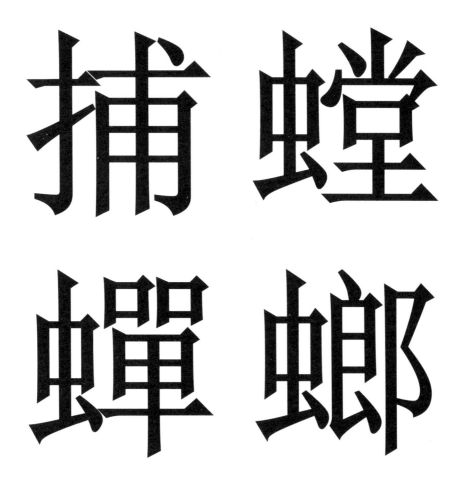

táng láng bǔ chán

(pronounced *tang lang boo charn*)

Literal meaning: mantis stalks cicada

Idiomatic meaning: to be so intent on doing something you don't notice the dangers involved

Here is another mantis chengyu from the philosopher Zhuangzi. There is a second half to this saying that translates as "the golden oriole waits behind". An adviser to the king of Wu used an even more extended version when the king was planning to attack Chu. He told the king that he had been in the garden and seen a mantis stalking a cicada, unaware of an oriole. The mantis caught the cicada but was caught in turn by the oriole. The minister then shot the oriole but didn't notice the pond behind him and tripped and fell in. The king took the hint and abandoned his plans.

tiān yī wú fèng

(pronounced *tien eee woo fung*)

Literal meaning: heaven's clothes without stitches

Idiomatic meaning: used to describe anything you can find no fault with;
a seamless argument; flawless

Chinese fairytales, particularly those written in the great Tang Dynasty (618–907), are full of encounters between men and beautiful immortals. The origin of this chengyu is the story of a young scholar called Guo Han. Unable to study in his room because of the heat and stuffy air, he goes outside to take a stroll. On his way he meets a beautiful girl wearing the most perfect clothes. He asks her how it can be that her clothes have no seams, and she replies that she is the Heavenly Weaver and the clothes she makes have no need of needle and thread.

tú qióng bǐ xiàn

(pronounced *too chyoong bee hsien*)

Literal meaning: map end dagger exposed

Idiomatic meaning: have nowhere to hide; be found out

This saying refers to one of the most famous incidents in Chinese history. As the First Emperor was slowly but surely conquering all the other states to unify China in the third century BCE, several attempts were made to assassinate him. He had offered a reward for the head of a disloyal general who had fled to another state. The general committed suicide so that an assassin, pretending to be a traitor, could take his head to the emperor along with a map showing the other states' defences. In the map was concealed a dagger to kill the emperor, but the plan failed when the emperor saw the dagger too soon.

wàng méi zhǐ kě

(pronounced *wong may jrrr cur*)

Literal meaning: look forward to plums stop thirst

Idiomatic meaning: feed on false hope

One of the most famous figures in Chinese history is Cao Cao (pronounced *tsow tsow*), last Chancellor of the Han Dynasty and ruler of the state of Wei in the Three Kingdoms Period (220–280). A renowned military strategist, he was famous for his ruthlessness and cunning. This saying derives from the story of how, when marching through a territory where all the wells had dried up, he soothed his soldiers' thirst by promising them that there was a huge orchard of plums over the next hill.

wáng yáng bǔ láo

(pronounced *wong yang boo lao*)

Literal meaning: lose sheep mend pen

Idiomatic meaning: lock the stable door after the horse has bolted

You only need to change the animal here and you have a famous English saying. The traditional Chinese story behind this saying involves a farmer whose sheep pen is damaged in a storm. His neighbours warn him that there is a wolf about and that he should mend the pen. The farmer ignores their advice and leaves it overnight. The next morning he has lost two of his sheep and only then does he repair the damage. Incidentally, in the Chinese version the animals involved could also be goats, because Chinese uses the same word for both.

wēi rú lěi luǎn

(pronounced *way roo lay lwan*)

Literal meaning: precarious as a pile of eggs

Idiomatic meaning: a dangerous situation; courting disaster; asking for trouble

The Duke of Ling decided to build himself an extravagant nine-storey ceremonial tower, even though it used up all the money for stocking the people's granaries and for paying the army. No one was allowed to complain. One of his ministers asked for an audience with the Duke and said: "Let me show you how I can balance nine duck eggs on twelve chess pieces," and proceeded to do so. "That is a really precarious tower," said the Duke. "Not as precarious as a tower that starves the people and angers your soldiers," the minister replied. The Duke was impressed by his subtlety and called a halt to the construction.

xìn kǒu cí huáng

(pronounced *hsin coe tsrr hwong*)

Literal meaning: randomly talk yellow arsenic

Idiomatic meaning: spout nonsense; talk rubbish

Yellow arsenic, also called yellow orpiment, was a mineral used in ancient times to cover over mistakes when writing. It seems that this chengyu derives from an earlier one in which a renowned scholar and orator was said to have orpiment in his mouth because he was so relaxed and eloquent that he could always correct any mistakes he made without hesitation. This led to the development of the chengyu above, which can also be extended to mean taking part in making false accusations.

之獻 忱曝

xiàn pù zhī chén

(pronounced *hsien poo jrrr chun*)

Literal meaning: offer warmth of the sun

Idiomatic meaning: polite words to use when giving a gift; it's nothing really; just a token gift

An old farmer spent the winter shivering with cold because he had neither warm clothes to wear nor firewood to burn to keep him warm. Gradually the weather began to improve as winter turned to spring and then summer. Finally it was warm enough for the farmer to sit outside and enjoy the heat of the sun's rays. He thought it was the most wonderful thing he had ever been given and decided that when the time of year came for the peasants to present their king with a gift, he would give the king the secret of sitting in the sun.

成胸竹有

xiōng yǒu chéng zhú

(pronounced *hsioong yo chung juw*)

Literal meaning: breast have created bamboo

Idiomatic meaning: see in one's mind's eye; have a clear picture;
to be sure of oneself

For many centuries bamboo has been one of the most favoured subjects for Chinese painters.
To achieve true mastery of it, however, the artist must spend months and years studying
bamboo in all its forms in different seasons and different places. In the end, he should be able
to paint bamboo with his eyes closed because he has, in his breast or mind's eye, a perfect
image of his subject.

xiǔ mù bù diāo

(pronounced *show moo boo dyow*)

Literal meaning: rotten wood can't be carved

Idiomatic meaning: you can't make a silk purse out of a sow's ear

This saying is an almost direct quotation from the *Analects* of Confucius, written in the fifth century BCE. In its original form it is the first half of a two-part sentence, which translates in full as "You can't carve rotten wood and you can't plaster a wall made of dung". This refers to Confucius' assertion that there are superior men and inferior men, and that only the superior man is able to follow the paths of Confucian virtue and become a true gentleman.

刺懸股梁

xuán liáng cì gǔ

(pronounced *hswan leeang tsr goo*)

Literal meaning: suspend beam prick thigh

Idiomatic meaning: to work really hard; to be dedicated to one's task

Long hours of hard study have always been the key to success in China. In ancient times people endeavoured to succeed in the examinations for entry and progress in the civil service, and in modern times people study to get into the best schools and universities. This saying refers to the lengths two particular scholars went to ensure they stayed awake. Sun Jing's technique was to tie his hair to a roof beam so he would be jerked awake if he nodded off. Su Qin more simply carried a thorn, which he would jab into his thigh if he felt sleepy.

yà miáo zhù zhǎng

(pronounced *ya miao joo jang*)

Literal meaning: pull shoots help grow

Idiomatic meaning: let things take their course; don't spoil things by interfering

This is a parable told by Mencius (372–289 BCE), the principal follower of Confucius. There once was an impatient farmer. He planted his seeds and went to the fields every day hoping that they had sprouted. When they finally did poke some shoots above the ground, he became irritated by how slowly they were growing and decided to do something to hurry them up. He spent all day taking every shoot and pulling it a little farther out of the ground. He went home well satisfied with his work, but when he returned the next day all the plants were dead.

yǎn ěr dào líng

(pronounced *yen er dao ling*)

Literal meaning: cover ears to steal a bell

Idiomatic meaning: bury one's head in the sand

This very popular chengyu is found in literature from the Tang Dynasty (618–907) onwards. According to the story, an incompetent thief tries to steal a huge golden bell from a temple. Having discovered it was too big for him to simply carry away, he decides to break it up with a sledgehammer. After he has heard the noise it makes the first time he hits it, he covers his ears with a scarf, thinking that if he can't hear it no one else can. He is quickly arrested.

白陽雪春

yáng chūn bái xuě

(pronounced *yang chwoon bye hsweh*)

Literal meaning: sun spring white snow

Idiomatic meaning: elegant and refined

Some of the seemingly simplest chengyu have the most complicated stories. In this case, 陽春白雪 is the name of a piece of music from the Warring States Period (476–221 BCE). A famous minister in the court of the king of Chu was summoned to the king's presence to answer criticisms of his conduct. The minister replied by comparing himself to a musician who played more and more elegant pieces of music so that those in the audience who truly appreciated them became fewer and fewer, leaving only the true connoisseurs. 陽春白雪 was the title of the last and finest piece he played.

yǎng hǔ yí huàn

(pronounced *yang hoo eee hwan*)

Literal meaning: raise tiger hand down disaster

Idiomatic meaning: always press home your advantage; don't give
your enemy a break

This is another story by Sima Qian, written towards the end of the Qin Dynasty (221–206 BCE)
and the beginning of the Han (206 BCE–220 CE). Liu Bang and Xiang Yu were fighting it
out for control of China. The struggle went one way and then another but finally Liu Bang
began to get the upper hand. Even so, he was still considering offering Xiang Yu a ceasefire.
However, one of his advisers said to him "Why offer Xiang Yu a treaty now? It would be like
raising a tiger and waiting for it to attack you." This convinced Liu Bang to change his mind
and he went on to defeat Xiang Yu and gain the empire.

yāng jí chí yú

(pronounced *yang gee chrrr ewe*)

Literal meaning: disaster reaches pond fish

Idiomatic meaning: describes an innocent bystander caught up
in a dangerous situation

This is a story from the *Spring and Autumn Annals*, the history of the state of Lu traditionally believed to have been compiled by Confucius. It is a parable about a greedy king who accidentally dropped a small jewel into the moat of his palace. Rather than lose even this tiny jewel, he ordered that the moat be drained and the peasants search the mud. They looked for a long time but did not find the jewel. In the meantime, all the fish in the moat died for lack of water.

yè cháng mèng duō

(pronounced *yeah charng mung dor*)

Literal meaning: long night many dreams

Idiomatic meaning: time brings many changes; there's many a slip
between cup and lip

Dreams are very important in Chinese philosophy, particularly in Buddhist teaching. In this saying, "dream" does not really have any of the connotations of hope or aspirations. Rather, as is frequently found in Buddhist teachings, it stands for the changing and impermanent nature of all things, and "night", in this instance, stands for human life. However, this saying admirably illustrates the many layers of a simple four-character phrase, because it may also been seen as a simple warning not to count one's chickens before they are hatched.

yī gǔ zuò qì

(pronounced *eee goo dzor chee*)

Literal meaning: one drum make spirit

Idiomatic meaning: in one fell swoop; to finish something at a stroke

This phrase first appears in the *Zuo Zhuan*, which, dating from early in the fourth century BCE, is the earliest surviving work of Chinese history. It comes in the description of a battle between the states of Qi and Lu. One of the Qi generals was about to order the drums to be beaten to signal the advance, but another general told him to wait until the enemy had struck their drums three times. The Qi army won a devastating victory and the second general later explained that the first time the drums are struck, the soldiers take courage, the second time they begin to waver and the third time they lose heart.

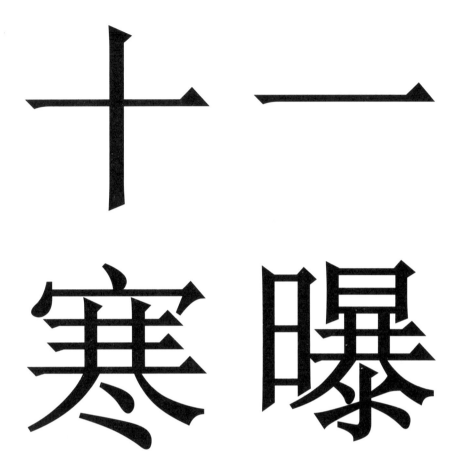

yī pù shí hán

(pronounced *eee poo shrr han*)

Literal meaning: one sunny ten cold

Idiomatic meaning: practice makes perfect; Rome wasn't built in a day;
there's no success without hard work

This comes from the writings of Mencius (372–289 BCE). Mencius was living in the court of
the king of Qi, who, although not dishonest, was easily led by corrupt ministers. He said to
the king: "All plants need sunlight to grow; if you keep them in the sun for only one day, and
in the dark for ten, they will not flourish." His meaning was that he knew it would be difficult
for the king because he, Mencius, could not stay with him long and that the corrupt courtiers
would be around much longer. Even so, the king should try to follow
the path of righteousness.

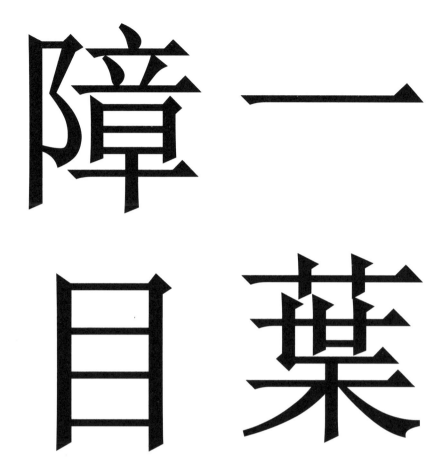

yí yè zhàng mù

(pronounced *eee yeah jang moo*)

Literal meaning: one leaf block eye

Idiomatic meaning: there is no direct English equivalent – see below

Some chengyu cannot easily be translated into English even though the meaning is so useful there really should be a direct English equivalent. In this story, a stupid farmer notices that a single leaf stops a bird from seeing an insect and eating it. He doesn't realize that it is a question of size, but rather believes that the leaf has the power to hide anything. He picks a leaf and takes it home thinking he can use it to disguise himself while he steals things. He is soon caught and put in prison. One mustn't assume that a part is the same as the whole.

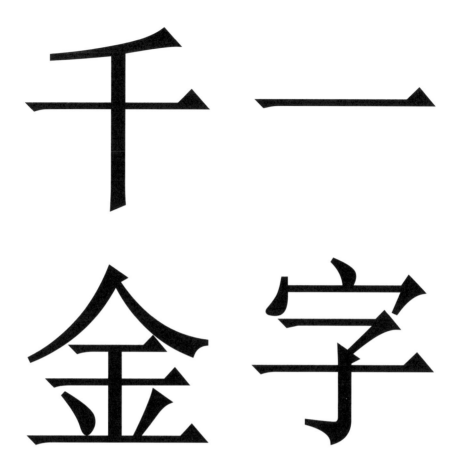

yī zì qiān jīn

(pronounced *eee dzrr chien jin*)

Literal meaning: one word a thousand pieces of gold

Idiomatic meaning: used to describe particularly fine and elegant writing

The origins of this chengyu are found in the greatest work of Chinese history, Sima Qian's *Records of the Grand Historian* written in the second to first centuries BCE. He tells how Lu Buwei, the man who helped the First Emperor gain power, commissioned thousands of scholars to write an encyclopedia of all knowledge. When it was finished it contained more than 200,000 characters. Lu believed it was so perfect he offered a reward of 1000 gold pieces if anyone could improve it even by even one character.

猶豫不決

yóu yù bù jué

(pronounced *you ewe boo joo-eh*)

Literal meaning: the "you" monkey can't decide

Idiomatic meaning: indecisive; caught in two minds; shilly-shally

The "you" is a type of monkey that is very timid and nervous. Any sound disturbs it and it immediately climbs up to the top of the highest and thickest tree, where it sits poking its head out until the coast is clear. It will then climb back down but is almost immediately scared again so it spends most of its day scuttling up and down trees and tiring itself out. No one seems to know exactly what kind of monkey this is, and most have forgotten that the character 猶 even refers to it, but the expression goes right back to the third century BCE or even earlier.

yù bàng xiāng zhēng

(pronounced *yew bung hsiang jeng*)

Literal meaning: snipe and crab fight each other

Idiomatic meaning: describes a quarrel that only serves to benefit a third party

This is another thoroughly useful saying that has no English equivalent, but really should do. This chengyu sometimes has a balancing second half that translates as "and the fisherman reaps the benefit". It is a cautionary tale of a clam that is sunning itself on the riverbank when a snipe flies down and catches it in its beak. The clam manages to clamp the bird's beak shut and the two stay there deadlocked, each unwilling to let go, until a fisherman comes along and takes them both home for his dinner.

yŭ hŭ móu pí

(pronounced *you hoo moe pee*)

Literal meaning: ask tiger seek skin

Idiomatic meaning: said of vainly asking someone to do something against their nature; you can't expect a leopard to change its spots

This chengyu also appears with a fox instead of a tiger being asked for its skin (the words sound very similar in Chinese). Its origins are lost but the story tells of a man who wanted a fur coat and went out to ask a tiger if it would give him its skin. No matter how many tigers he asked, he was unsuccessful. The saying was most famously used by Dr Sun Yat-sen (1866–1925), who was revered by the Chinese as the Father of the Nation. He wrote that asking the Western powers in Asia peacefully to return power to the Chinese was like asking a tiger for its skin.

yuè xià lǎo rén

(pronounced *you-eh hsia lao wren*)

Literal meaning: old man under the moon

Idiomatic meaning: play cupid; act as match-maker

A general of the Tang Dynasty (618–907) came across an old man sitting in the moonlight reading a big thick book. The general asked the man what he was reading. The man replied that it was the book of all marriages and that he could control who married whom. "That little girl sleeping over there will be your wife," the man said. The general flew into a rage, and ordered one of his soldiers to kill the little girl. However, the soldier took pity on the girl and only made a small cut between her eyebrows. Years later, the general married the young daughter of a provincial governor, whose beauty was only spoiled by a scar between her eyebrows.

zhài tái gāo zhù

(pronounced *jye tie gow joo*)

Literal meaning: debt platform high build

Idiomatic meaning: up to one's neck in/buried under a mountain of debt

Sima Qin used this chengyu in his *Records of the Grand Historian*, which he wrote in the second to first centuries BCE. The king of Chu persuaded Zhou Nan, the last head of the fading Zhou Dynasty, that Qin was weakening and now was the time to strike. Zhou Nan believed him and borrowed huge sums of money from his nobles to finance his army. In the end, only two other states joined the attack against Qin and they were easily defeated. The nobles all came to Zhou Nan's palace demanding their money back. However, he could not pay them and fled to the top of his ceremonial platform to hide from them.

zhāo sān mù sì

(pronounced *jao san moo srrr*)

Literal meaning: morning three night four

Idiomatic meaning: there's one born every minute; a fool and his money are easily parted; play someone for a sucker

According to a story told by the philosopher Zhuangzi, who lived in the fourth century BCE, the Master of the Monkeys became concerned that there were too many monkeys and his supply of food too little. He decided to ration the monkeys and went to tell them the bad news. "From now on," he said, "I shall give you four bowls in the morning and three at night." The monkeys were furious and complained bitterly. "Oh, very well," the master said. "I'll give you three in the morning and four at night." At that the monkeys went away satisfied, thinking they had got more than the first offer.

zhī lù wéi mǎ

(pronounced *jrrr loo way ma*)

Literal meaning: point at a deer call it a horse

Idiomatic meaning: swear that black is white; the emperor's new clothes

The origin of this saying is a Chinese variant of the tale of the Emperor's New Clothes. In the court of the Second Emperor, there was an ambitious minister, Zhao Gao, who hoped to usurp the throne. In order to identify those other ministers still loyal to the emperor, he presented him with a deer, claiming it was a beautiful horse. The emperor did not believe him, but Zhao Gao's followers also insisted it was a horse. Only those loyal to the emperor still called it a deer, and Zhao Gao took note of their names and then disposed of them one by one.

zhì zǐ yí lín

(pronounced *jrrr dzrr eee lin*)

Literal meaning: clever son suspicious neighbour

Idiomatic meaning: always keep an open mind; don't just trust the familiar

This is another example of a chengyu that can be approximately translated into English, but there is no real equivalent with the same subtlety of meaning. It is a story dating from the Song Dynasty (960–1279) about a man whose discovers that the fence around his property has been damaged in a storm. His son warns him that he should mend it immediately or else thieves might get in. His neighbour too gives him the same advice. That night, the property is indeed burgled. The man's immediate reaction is to praise his son's intelligence for predicting this, and to suspect his neighbour of committing the crime.

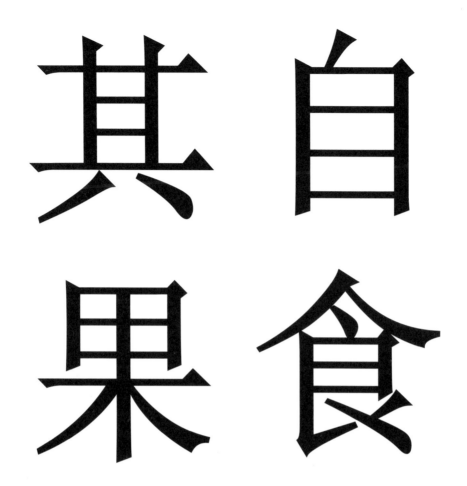

zì shí qí guǒ

(pronounced *dzrr chrr chee gwor*)

Literal meaning: self eat own fruit

Idiomatic meaning: reap what you have sown; get your just desserts;
a taste of your own medicine

Some stories traditionally ascribed to chengyu seem to be there for form's sake, not because there is any direct relationship. This very straightforward saying is given a long story about a monk and a young man, which is simply an illustration rather than a source. A young man is upset when a monk ignores him in favour of a wealthier traveller. The monk explains that, in fact, he pays more attention to those he does not respect, because those he does have no need of flattery. The young man then beats the monk with a stick explaining that he only hits people he likes.

zì xiāng máo dùn

(pronounced *dzrr hsiang mao dwun*)

Literal meaning: self-opposing spear and shield

Idiomatic meaning: a contradiction in terms; beat oneself with one's own staff

This is one of the most widely used chengyu. Its explanation is first found in a story told by the philosopher Han Fei in his book, entitled *Han Fe Zi*, written in the third century BCE. There he describes a stallholder in a market selling both spears that can penetrate anything and shields that cannot be pierced by anything. When challenged about this contradiction, he had no answer. In contemporary mandarin, 矛盾 (máo dùn) now simply means a contradiction or a problem.

Glossary of principal people and texts

Confucius: The most famous ancient Chinese sage-philosopher lived from 551–479 BCE during the period of the *Spring and Autumn Annals* in Qufu, modern Shandong province. His philosophy, recorded in the *Analects*, and expanded upon by disciples such as Mencius, covers both moral and political ethics. It is based upon the obligation of individuals to act on the rights and responsibilities appropriate to their station, and the proper observance of rites and ritual. Its guiding principles are those of 仁 *rén* (benevolence) and 義 *yì* (righteousness). He is also, by tradition, the author or editor of the Five Classics of ancient Chinese literature which include the *Spring and Autumn Annals* that give the period of his birth its name.

Laozi: Second only to Confucius in his fame as an ancient Chinese philosopher, Laozi traditionally lived at approximately the same time as Confucius, in the Sixth Century BCE. He is the author of the *Daodejing* (*Tao Te Ching*) and, because of this, revered as the founder of the Daoist religion in China and one of its principal deities. There is in fact debate over whether a single person called Laozi actually existed. He remains, however, the most influential figure in the development of the early forms of both Daoism and Buddhism, which was initially interpreted in China through Daoist ideas. The opening sentences of the *Daodejing* are amongst the most enigmatic and debated of all literature.

Shuihu Zhuan: Best known in the west in its translation as *The Water Margin*, also a cult Japanese TV series in the 1970s, Shuihu Zhuan is one of the four classic novels of the Chinese literature, along with *Honglou Meng* (*Dream of the Red Chamber*), *San Guo Yanyi* (*Romance of the Three Kingdoms*) and *Xiyou Ji* (*Journey to the West*). It was written in the Fourteenth Century, principally by Shi Naian, about whom very little is known. Often described as a Chinese version of Robin Hood, it tells of the adventures of 108 outlaws of the Song Dynasty in the marshlands around Mt Liang in Shandong Province. The stories are developed from the deeds of a group of actual outlaws recorded in the History of the Song Dynasty. Some of the characters such as Song Jiang, Wu Song and Lu Zhishen, are amongst the most popular figures in Chinese literature and still figure in film and television today.

Sima Qian: Known as the Grand Historian of China, he lived between 145–86 BCE in the Han Dynasty (206 BCE–220 CE). He is the author of the *Shi Ji* (*Historical Records*), the greatest historical work of Chinese literature, which covers Chinese history from its mythical beginnings with the Yellow Emperor to his own time under the Han Emperor Wudi. It was, amongst other things, the principle source of information about the First Emperor, Qinshihuang, until recent archaeological discoveries have begun to shed new light. Sima Qian was so devoted to his work as a historian that, when convicted of sedition against Emperor Wudi, he chose to suffer castration rather than execution in order to finish his book.

Zhan Guo Ce: The *Strategies of the Warring States* was compiled between the late Fourth and First centuries BCE. It partially documents the history of the Warring States period between 490 BCE and the unification of the Empire under the first Emperor, Qinshihuang, in 221 BCE. It is an important source of historical, political and social information about the period and provides the basis for many popular stories and proverbs still current today.

Zhuangzi: This is both the name of an important Daoist text, and the honorific title of its author Zhuang Zhou, who lived in the Fourth Century BCE. It is by no means certain that Zhuangzi composed the whole work, but he is generally credited with its core chapters. Although the book has been adopted as a Daoist classic, Zhuangzi is not overtly a Daoist philosopher. He is both a sceptic and a relativist and writes very beautifully, though sometimes impenetrably, about the relationship between life and knowledge. In one of the most famous passages, Zhuangzi dreams he is a butterfly unaware of his existence as a human. When he wakes up and is Zhuangzi once more, he can no longer be sure whether he is indeed Zhuangzi, or a butterfly dreaming he is Zhuangzi.

Zuo Zhuan: The *Chronicle of Zuo* is the one of the earliest surviving historical Chinese texts and was compiled in the late Fifth and early Fourth centuries BCE. It is attributed to Zuo Qiuming, but this is by no means certain. It records the history of the 12 dukes of the State of Lu beween 772–468 BCE. The state of Lu, corresponding to part of the modern province of Shandong, was also the home of Confucius and its rulers also the subject matter of the *Spring and Autumn Annals* which Confucius is believed to have edited. The clear and precise style of the Zuo Zhuan provided a model for generations of Chinese historians and the work also furnished us with much important information about its period.

Dynastic chronology of Chinese history

Dates	Dynasty	Chinese Translation
ca. 2000–1500 BCE	Xia	夏
1700–1027 BCE	Shang	商
1027–771 BCE	Western Zhou	西周
	Eastern Zhou	東
770–221 BCE	770–476 BCE Spring and Autumn period	春秋時代
	475–221 BCE Warring States period	戰國時代
221–207 BCE	Qin	秦
	Western Han	西漢
206 BCE–220 CE	Xin (9–24 CE)	新
	Eastern Han	东漢
220–280 CE	Three Kingdoms	三國
265–316	Western Jin	西晉
317–420	Eastern Jin	東晉
420–588	Southern and Northern Dynasties	南北朝
581–617	Sui (*pronounced: sway*)	隨
618–907	Tang	唐
907–960	Five Dynasties	五代
907–979	Ten Kingdoms	十國
	Song (*pronounced: soong*)	宋
960–1279	960–1127 Northern Song	北宋
	1127–1279 Southern Song	南宋
916–1125	Liao	辽
1115–1234	Jin	金
1279–1368	Yuan	元
1368–1644	Ming	明
1644–1911	Qing (*pronounced: ching*)	清
1911–1949	Republic of China	中華民國
1949–	People's Republic of China	中华人民 共和国

Index